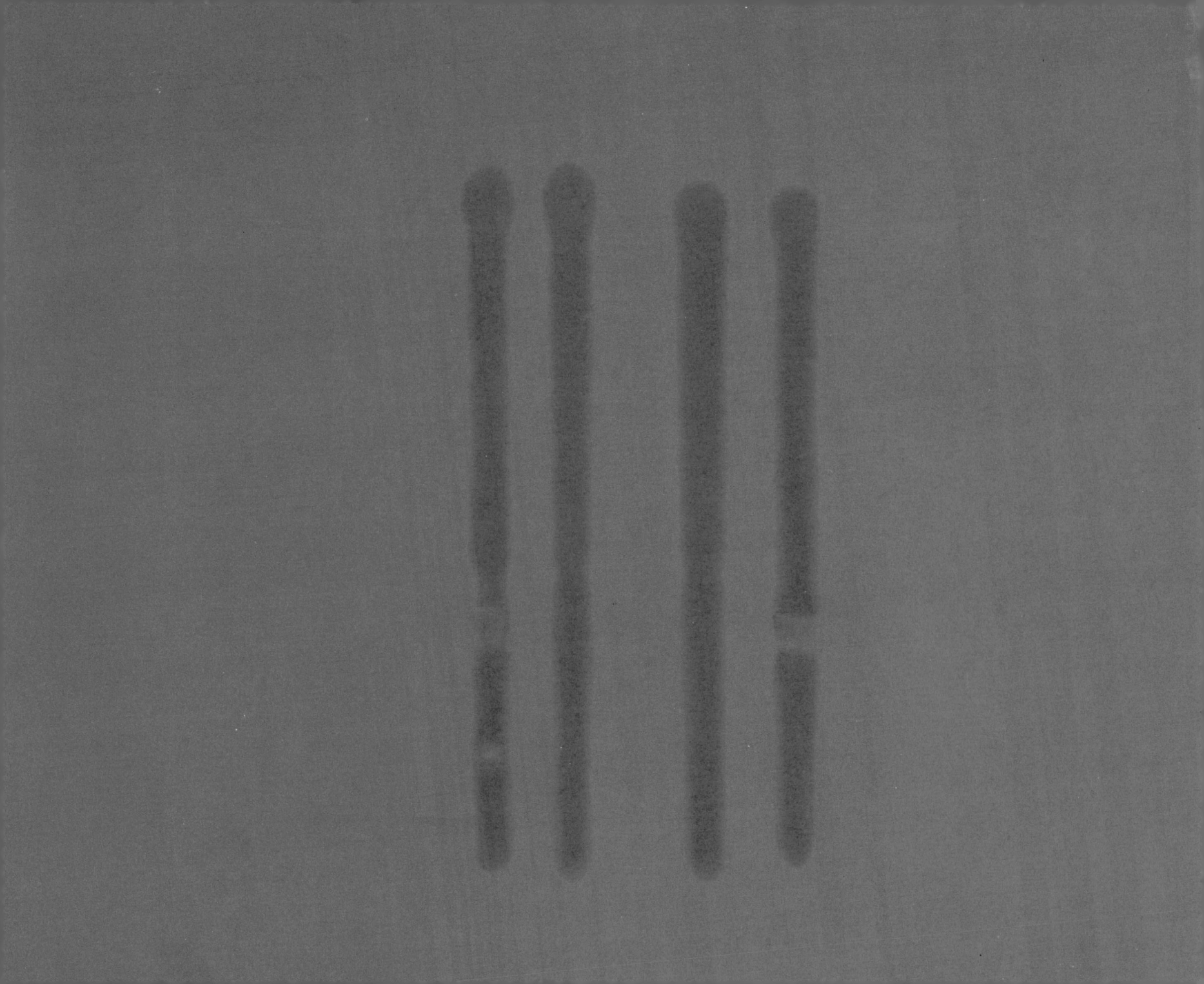

MOONSNACKS
AND ASSORTED NUTS

MOONSNACKS

Someone ate the Moon last night
And left only a crest,
I wonder if he'll come tonight
And eat up all the rest?
I wonder if it tasted like
A great, big cheese balloon?
Do you suppose somehow last night
A mouse got on the Moon?

GREENE BARK PRESS, INC.
P.O. Box 1108
Bridgeport, CT 06601-1108

POEMS BY MARY GRACE DEMBECK
ILLUSTRATIONS BY JEAN PIDGEON

ISBN 1-880851-11-3

Published by Greene Bark Press Inc.
P.O. Box 1108
Bridgeport, CT 06601-1108

CONTENTS

Moonsnacks	1
Gadzook Tea	4
Tutti Frutti Lovesong	9
*Handy Footnote	10
First Halloween on Mars *(On Occasion of the Invasion of Earthlings)*	12
Mum's The Word	14
Bedtime Story	17
Jilly Janet Kelly *(A jump rope rhyme)*	19
Noah's Wife	20
Same Difference	25
When Mama Cooks	26
The Bread and Butter / Batter Battle	28
Invitation	30
Contrary Mary	33
Sweet Dream	35
A Day in the Life Of Bryant the Giant	36
Poems	40

GADZOOK TEA

A witch, feeling lonely for company,
Invited some neighbors to come at three,
She made Lizard Scones
And Tart Jelly Bones,
And brewed a big cauldron of Gadzook Tea.

Her door gong sounded, she shrieked with glee,
There, on her stair, stood her company,
A dragon, two rats,
Three snakes and four bats,
Five spiders, six toads and a chimpanzee.

"Creep in!", cried the witch, "You are right on time…
I just finished boiling a bucket of slime,
To go with my scones
And Tart Jelly Bones!"
"Oh, good!", hissed a snake, "They're all favorites of mine!"

They crawled and they crept to their usual places,
And tied on their napkins of cobwebby laces,
The witch served them each
With a howl and a screech,
And they slurped as they filled up their horrible faces.

4

The dragon was first to get sick, was he,
Then the rats, snakes and bats
And the chimpanzee,
The spiders went plop,
As the toads fell on top,
Tipping over the cauldron of Gadzook tea.

Weeks later they woke up and growled, "Your tea's
The worst thing you've made us since Scrambled Fleas!"
The witch blushed bright red,
"Why, thank you!", she said,
"I'm so glad you liked it. I try to please."

"Do make it again!" they all yelled with a roar,
"It was so disgusting!", they cried, "We want more!"
 She brewed up a lot, They each drank a pot,
"Enjoy!", shrieked the witch as they sank to the floor.

The witch never lacks now for company,
Her neighbors moved in with her, one, two, three...
Just go by some night,
You'll hear shrieks of delight
As they guzzle down gallons of Gadzook Tea.

Tea End

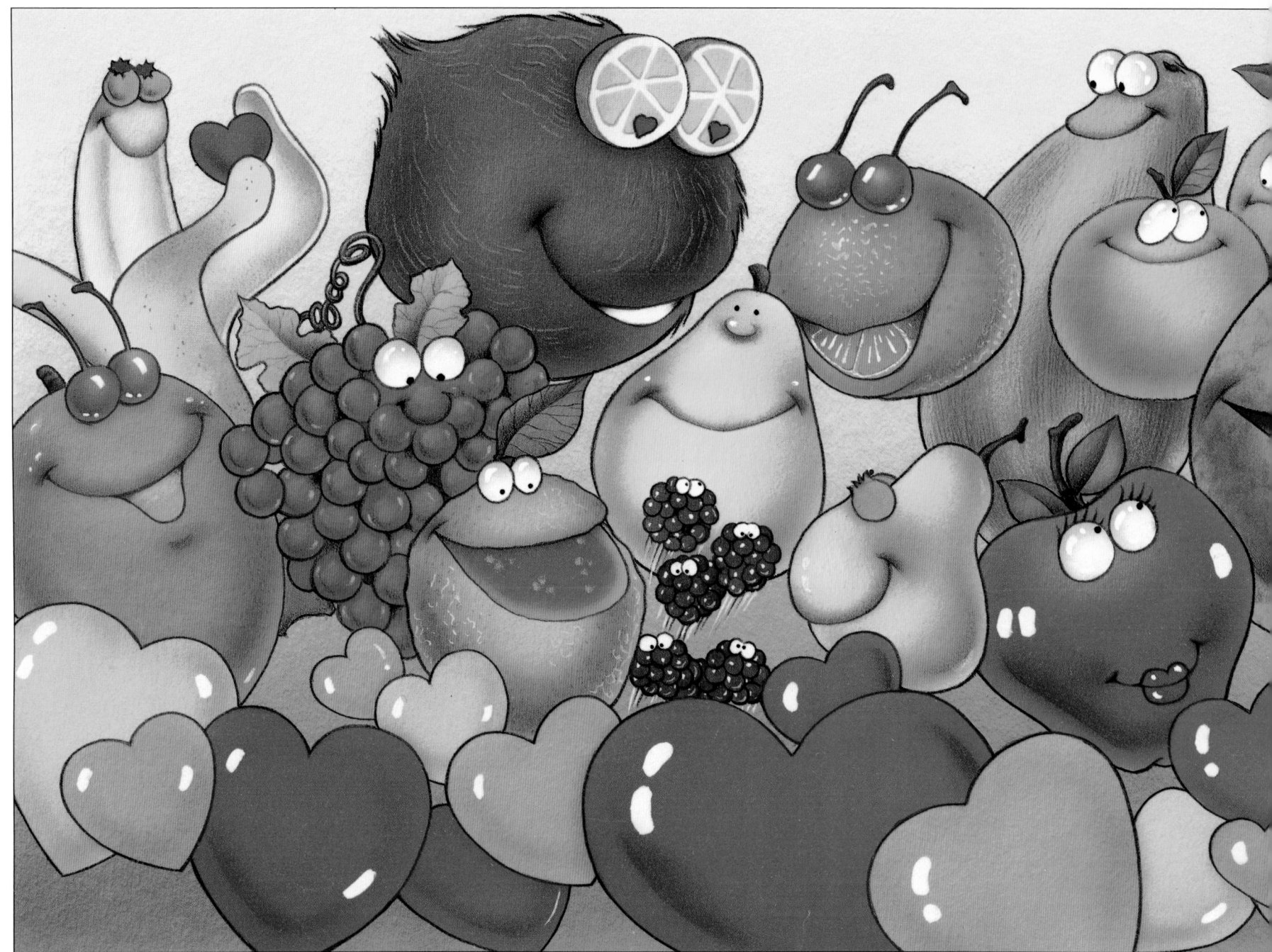

Tutti Frutti Lovesong

You are my darling CUMQUAT,
Oh, you're my PEACHy pie,
I think you are the BERRIES,
The APPLE of my eye.

Don't make me MELON-choly,
Please be my HONEY DEW,
'Cause oh, my sweet PAPAYA.
I'm BANANAS over you!

I would be oh, so GRAPEful
If you'd just say you care,
For it takes two to MANGO,
And we're a PEACHy PEAR.

Oh, ORANGE you a little
COCONUTS for me too?
Please say you'll be mon CHERRY,
I'm so GUAVA over you.

9

I wrote a note to my Right Foot,
Inviting it to tea,
And when my Left Foot heard the news,
It got mad at me.
"Just because I'm never Right…"
It told me with a pout,
"Is no reason you should go
And make me feel Left out!"

*Well, I have learned a lesson,
To keep a feud from brewing,
I never let my Left Hand
Know what my Right Hand's doing.

10

FIRST HALLOWEEN ON MARS
(On the occasion of the invasion of Earthlings)

I'm not answering my front door,
Not getting scared like I got before . . .
A creature of a shape and size
And color I don't recognize
Is jumping out before my eyes
And hollering "Trick or treat!"

My antennae are frazzled through and through,
My wings are sagging, my horns are too,
My heads are aching, my eyes are sore,
My tails cannot wag anymore,
Be still my hearts! . . . Just hear them beat
Whenever "IT" yells "Trick or treat!"

There goes the doorbell . . . I'll just peek,
Oh, no! . . . it has just ONE head . . . EEEK!
It's bare, without one single scale,
Or one antenna, wing or tail,
And just two arms and just two feet,
And one mouth hollering "Trick or treat!"

Oh, won't this nightmare ever end?
What I need most now is a friend,
Someone normal, just like me,
With three heads where three heads should be,
Right above its ten big feet,
And not hollering, "Trick or treat!"

MUM'S THE WORD

I bought a Mum plant at the store,
The best I'd ever seen,
Its stems were straight,
Its roots were strong,
Its leaves were thick and green.
I kept it moist,
I gave it light,
I did all that I could,
To help my Mum grow big and bright,
The way a mum plant should.
I sang it songs,
I told it tales,
I did not leave its side,
I talked,
    And talked,
        And talked,
            Until
It got so bored it died!

*Published in February, 1991, National Wildlife Federation's Ranger Rick magazine.

BEDTIME STORY

So you want a story,
You want me to tell
Of the awful Lump-Bumps
Who dwell down a well?
To tell of the Nasties
That eat everyone,
And to please make it scary,
Because it's more fun!
You want me to tell
Of the Crawlies that creep,
Of the Brawlies that keep you
From falling asleep?
So you want a good fright
And a nice chill or two?...
Well, how about if
I just simply say
BOO!

JILLY JANET KELLY
(A jump rope rhyme)

Jilly
Janet Kelly
Had a dilly
Of a bean,
And she put it
In her pocket
So to keep it
Nice and clean!
Now that Jilly
Janet Kelly's
Bean was made of
Jilly Jelly —
'Twas a dilly,
Of a Jilly
Janet Kelly
Jelly bean!

After she scrubbed down the walls,
Swabbed the decks and swept the stalls,
Cleaned the windows, waxed the rails,
Starched and ironed all the sails,
Pulled the mizzenmast up high,
Hung out all the wash to dry,
Made the beds for sleep that night,
Made the Ark all shiny bright,
What did Mrs. Noah do,
When on board came, two by two,
Lions, tigers, birds and monkeys,
Squirrels, elephants and donkeys,
Cows and frogs and kangaroos,
Leaping, kicking, mooing moos…
Pushing, squshing, scrapping, squalling,
Neighing, braying, caterwauling,
 Leaving a great big mess behind,
Didn't Mrs. Noah mind?

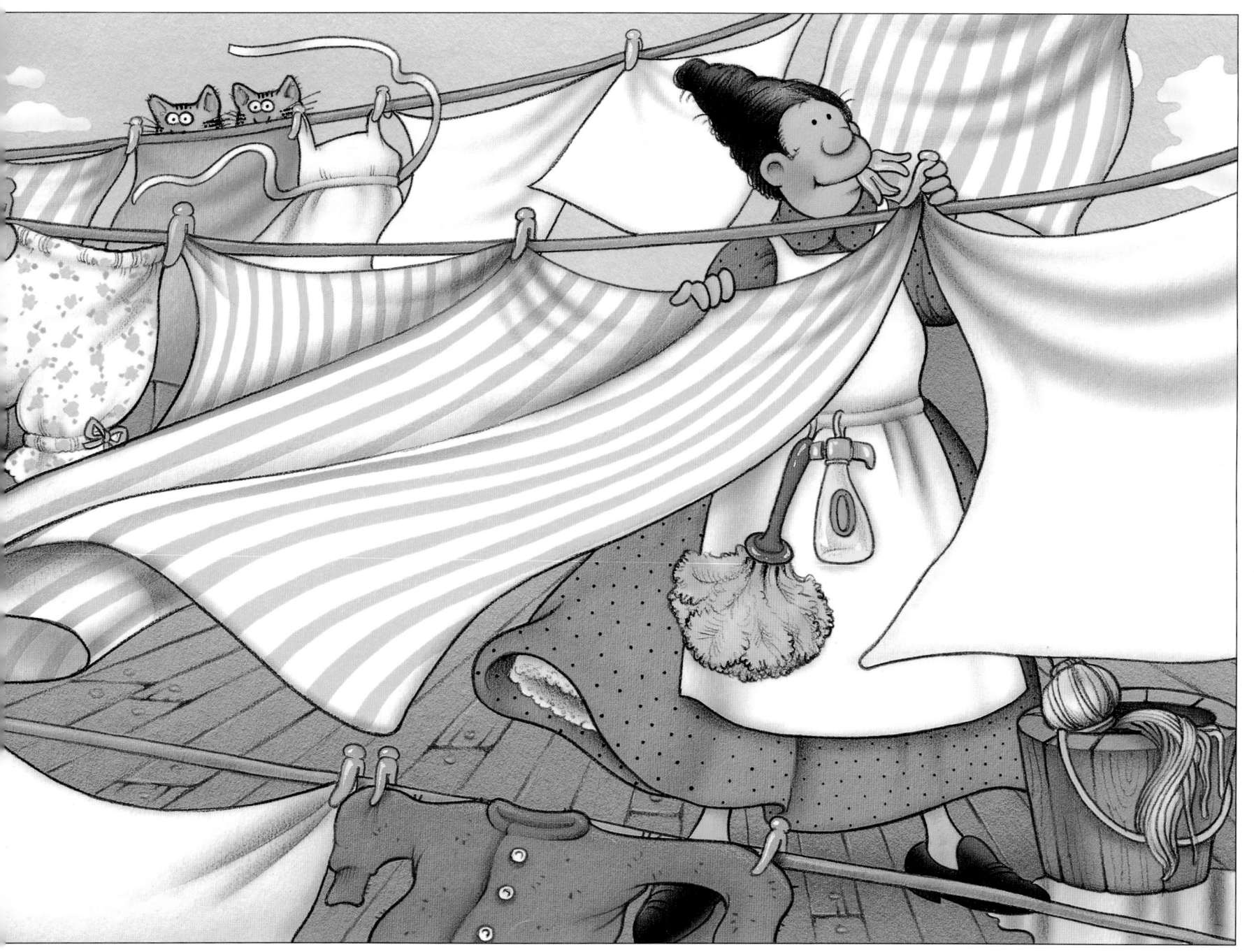

Did she cry, "Whoa! I quit!
Really, Noah, this is it!
The swine are pigs!
The snakes are vipers!
The baby elephants need diapers!
The mice are rats!
The snails are slugs!
The bees and fleas just drive me bugs!"
And on and on,
From dawn to dark,
Until poor Noah parked the Ark?

SAME DIFFERENCE

Little wee Lee Lolly Lynne,
Has a sister, Lou, her twin,
Dressed the same,
From head to toes,
Which is Lee?
Which Lou?
Who knows?

Lee looks lovely,
So does Lou,
But I can't tell
Who is who,
Till I meet them
Both and say:
"Hi! How are
You two today?"

When one says:
"Good as can be!"
And one says:
"Don't bother me!"
Then I know
Just who is who...
The nice one's Lee,
The grouch is Lou!

25

WHEN MAMA COOKS

When Mama cooks a stew for us,
She always makes a lot,
She likes to throw all sorts of things
Into a big, black pot.
She adds some gloop, she adds some glop,
She adds a bunch of gross,
Then
Bubble,
Bobble,
Bibble,
Boil!
She adds another dose.
And very soon it starts to smell
So yummy and delitch,
That's when we are the gladdest that
Our Mama is
A witch!

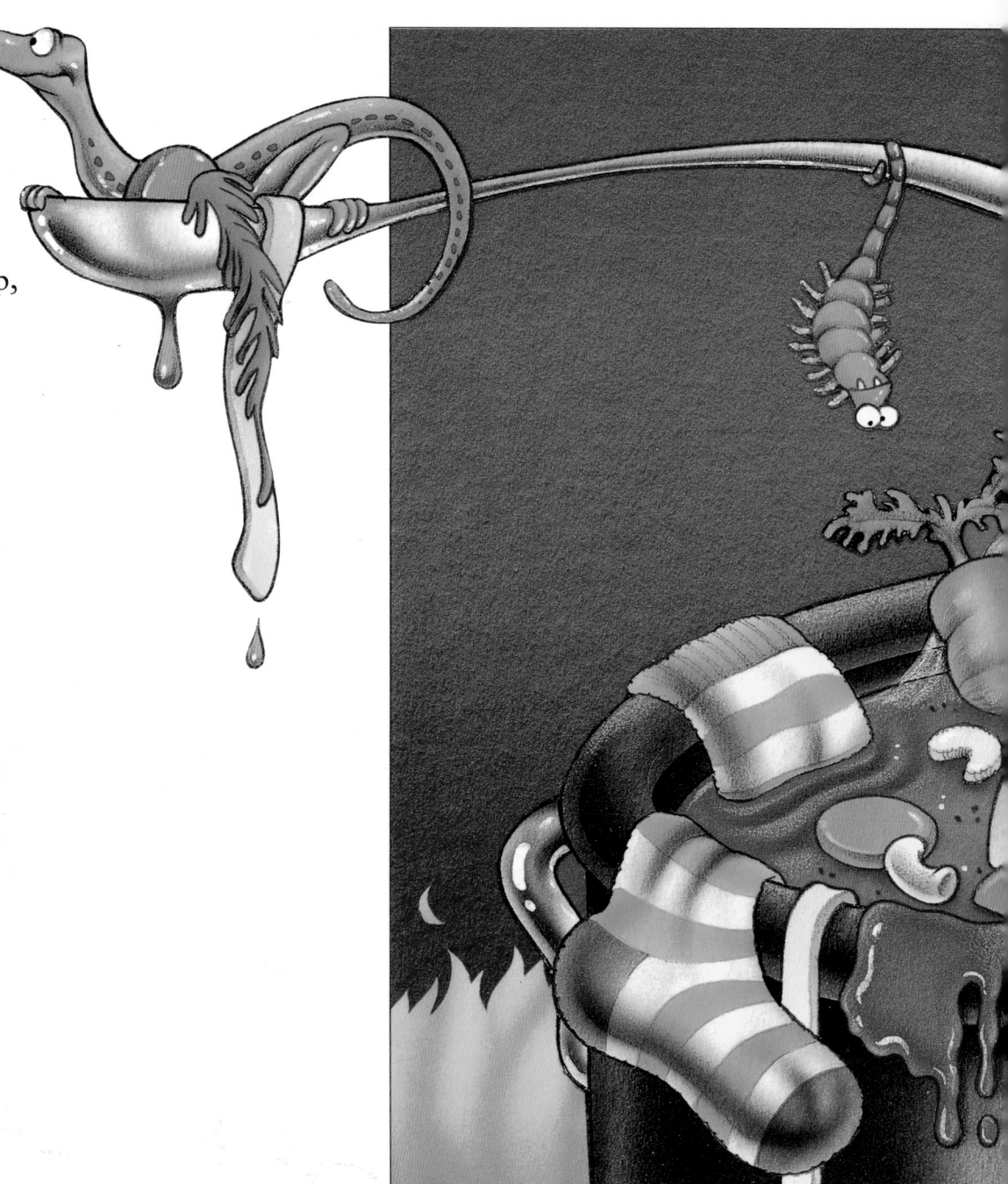

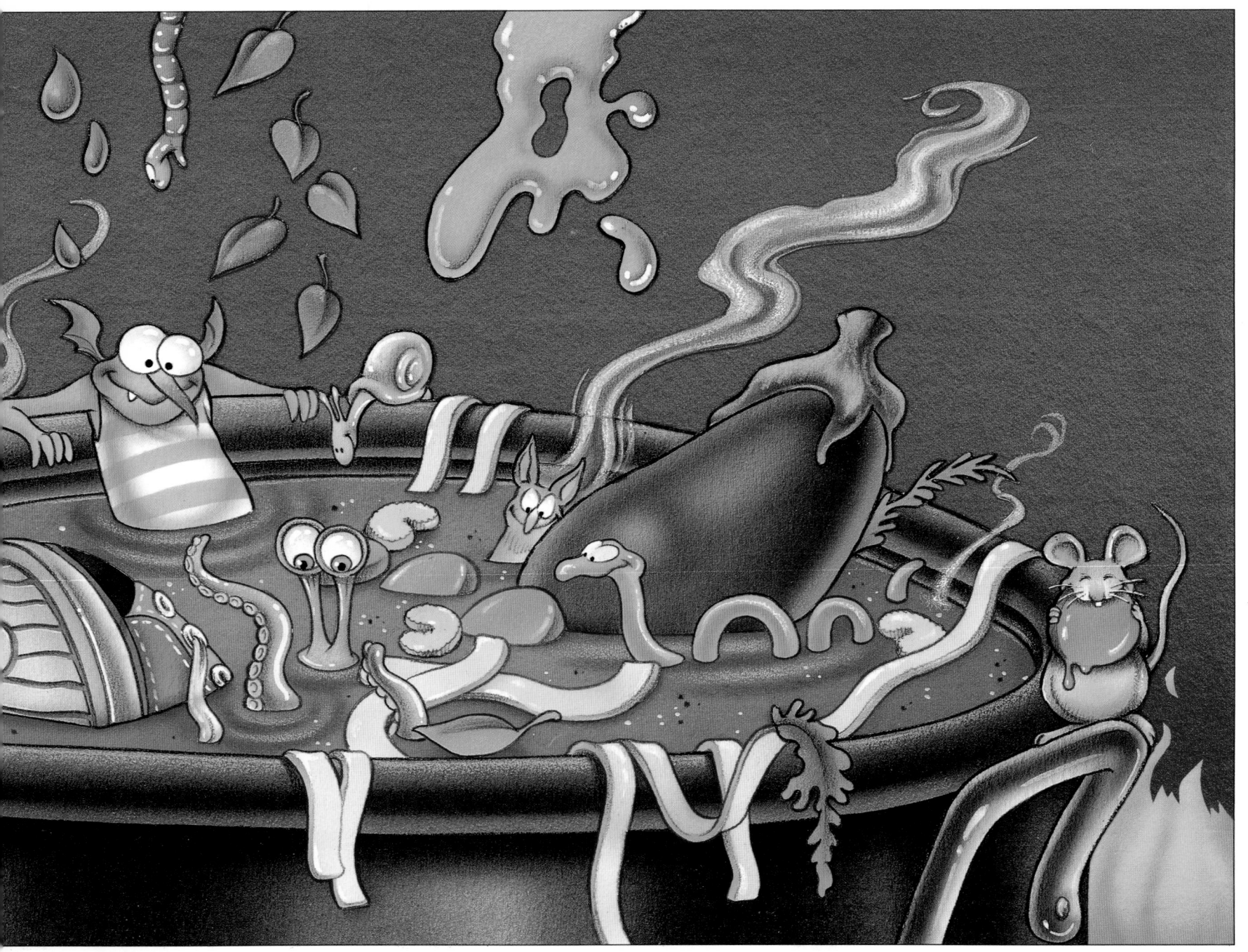

My brother likes butter,
While I prefer batter
My brother eats butter
With bread, but no matter,
My mother eats batter
With bread, but no butter,
And then there's my father
Who goes even further...
 My father eats butter
With big globs of batter,
(He'd eat it with bread but
'Twould make father fatter.)
So, all day we battle,
Each one with the other,
About which is better,
Bread, batter or butter.

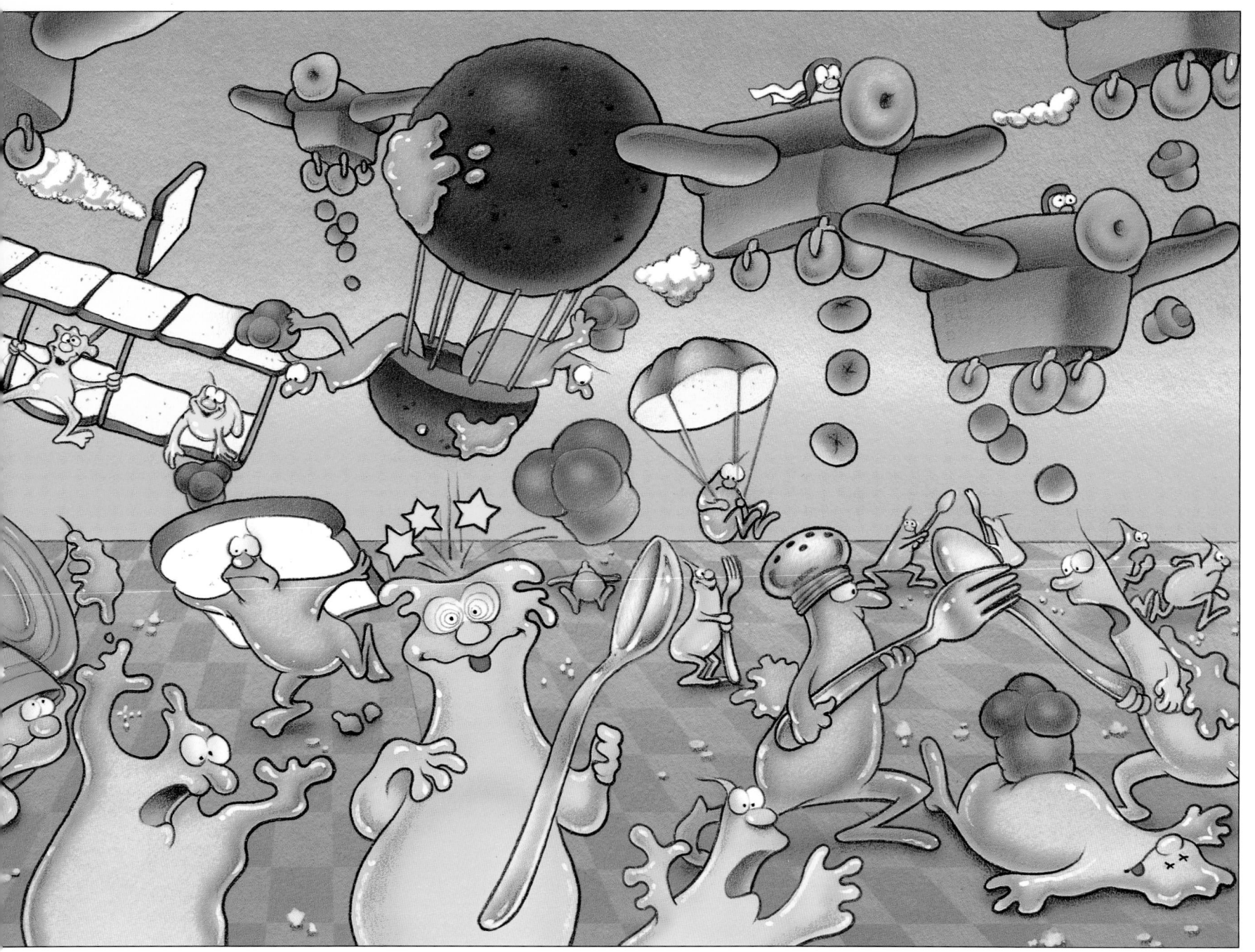

INVITATION

If you like your eggs all runny,
If you like toast charcoal brown,
Come to my house, my dad's cooking,
'Cause my mom is out of town.

If you like your white socks colored,
If you like clothes with a streak,
Bring your laundry, my dad's washing,
'Cause my mom's been gone a week.

All our sinks are piled with dishes,
And we've burned up all our pans,
And we're eating with our fingers,
And we're drinking coke from cans.

And we're having week old pizza
For our lunch and dinner too,
But our dad, (who is a health nut),
Makes us scrape off the green goo.

If you like watching t.v. late
And no scolding when you're bad,
Better come before my mom's home,
She's not half as fun as dad.

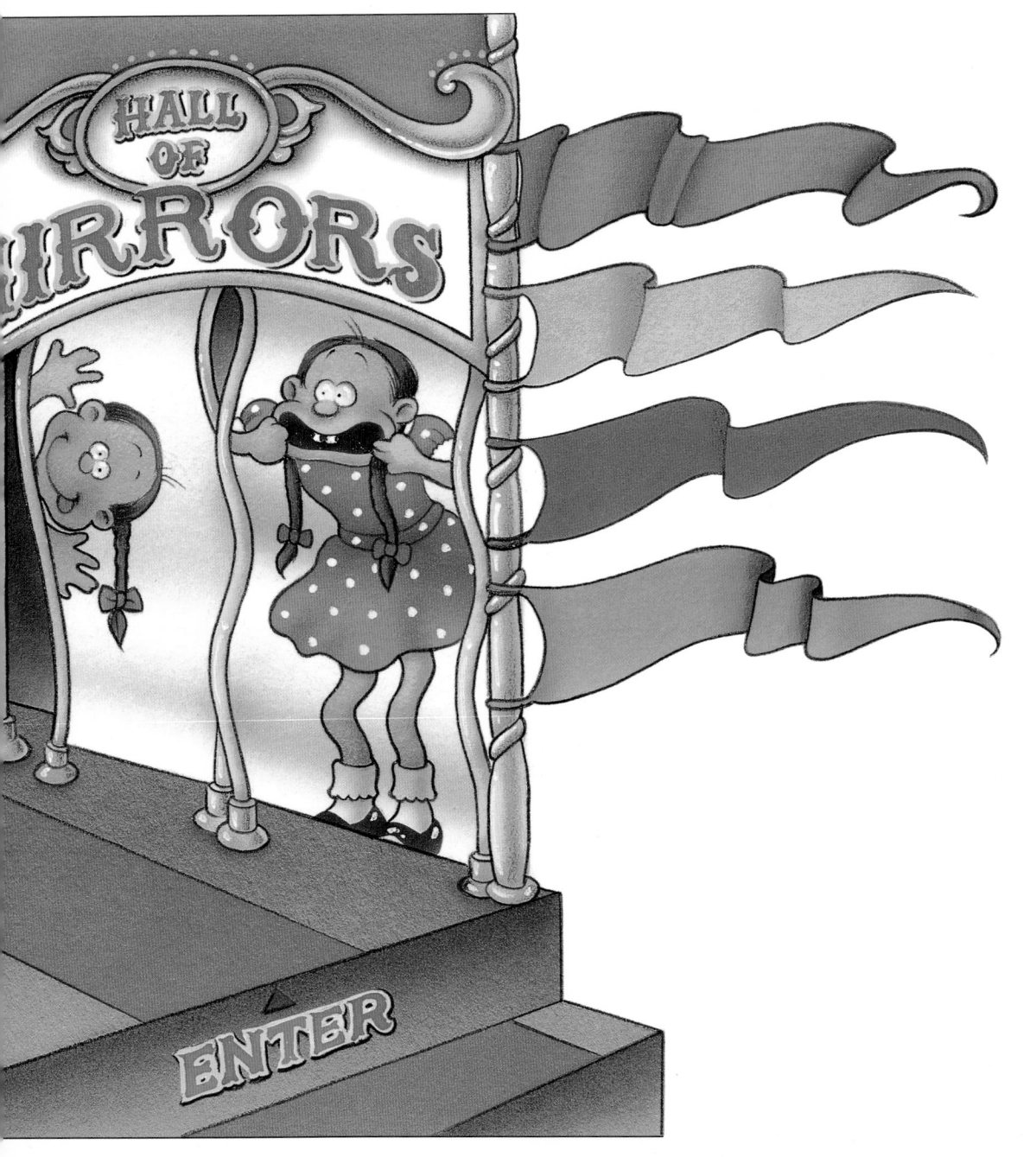

CONTRARY MARY

Inside she's a Gypsy girl,
Outside, soft and sweet,
Inside she is whacky, wild,
Outside prim and neat,
Inside she's a dinosaur,
Outside, just a puppy,
Inside she's a tiger-shark,
Outside, just a guppy...
But be careful,
Lest she pout
And turns herself
Inside out!

SWEET DREAM

I dreamed up a grandma
All plumpy and sweet,
Who loved to bake brownies
That I loved to eat.
She'd let me taste anything
That she was cooking
And slipped me some nickels
When no one was looking.
She'd always stick up for me
In times of trouble.
And though I just loved her,
She'd love me back double.
She'd always be there for me
Asking "What's new?"
And there wasn't anything
She wouldn't do
To comfort or cheer me up
On a hard day,
To her I was perfect,
In every which way.
I dreamed up this grandma
And suddenly knew
It wasn't a dream,
Grandma dear,
It was you.

35

Bryant awakes and he stokes up the sun,
Takes a bath in the ocean
And after he's done,
He tramps to his kitchen and starts to beat
A thousand scrambled eggs to eat.
Then off he goes on his daily stroll,
Ten giant steps and he's reached the Pole,
Splashing his way through icy seas,
He crosses the Alps and the Pyrenees,
Puffing his pipe as he lumbers by,
Blowing huge clouds across the sky.
Next, a left turn, and he's trudging south
Straightening swamps and jungles out,
Brushing off lions and tigers who feel
A big, burly giant would make a great meal.

Soon it gets late... night has begun
With one mighty puff, he blows out the sun,
Pins up the moon, straightens the stars
And planets, like Pluto and Venus and Mars.
Once 'round the world he goes and then
Bryant, the Giant, is home again,
Eats fifty pizzas with peppers and cheese,
And, for dessert, ten banana fruit trees.
With one giant yawn, along about ten,
He gets in pajamas and washes up, then,
Leaving his clothes in a big, giant heap,
He jumps into bed with a big giant leap,
Falls fast asleep in his big, giant lair,
With a big giant hug
For his toy teddy bear.

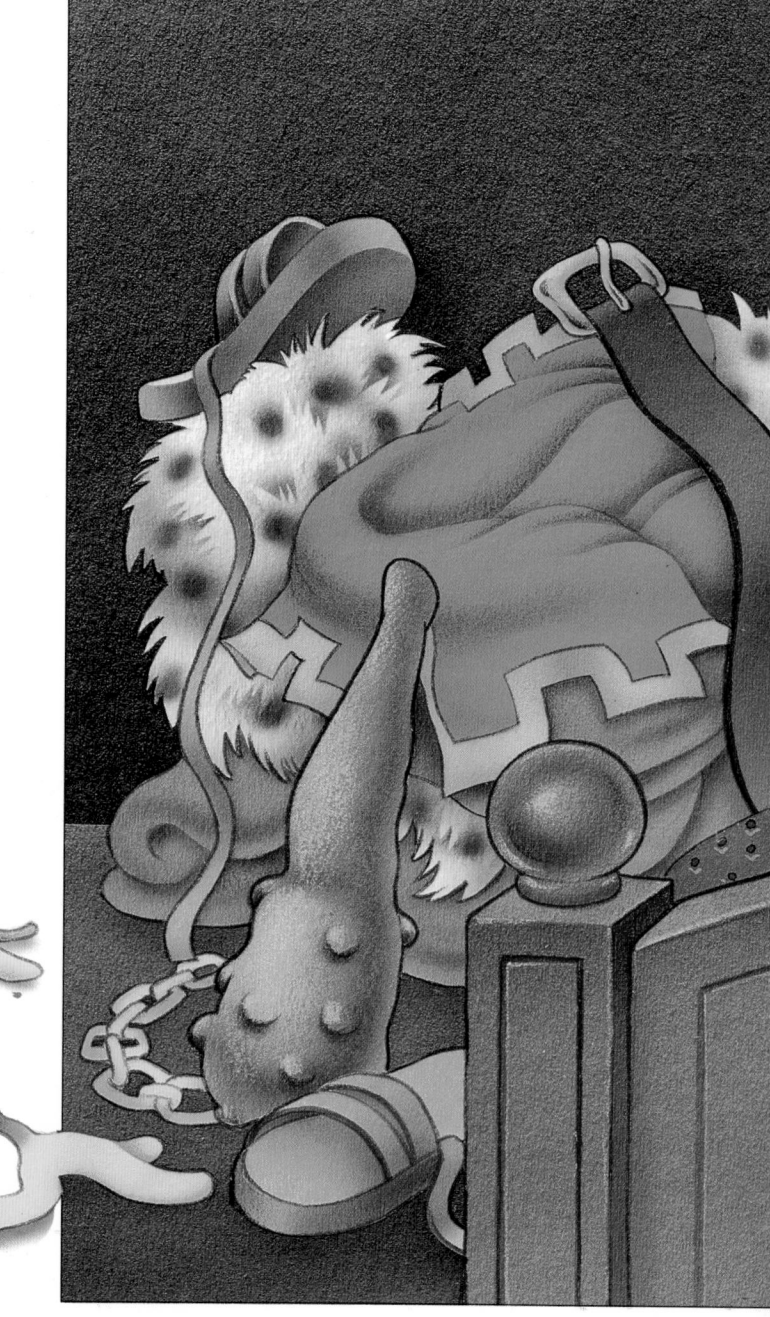

POEMS

Poems are thought makers
Or they're just fun,
Some end in rhyme
But this isn't one
Of those.